Copyright 2018 by Kevin Mitanidis

All Rights Reserved

All rights reserved. No part of this publication may be reproduced or transmitted in any form or by any means, electronically, or mechanically, including photocopy, recording, or by any information storage and retrieving system without permission from the publisher.

For further information or request for permission to make copies of any part of the work should be written form and mailed to the following address.

To contact us:

e-mail question@fasteasylaw.com

Fasteasylaw.com

First edition 2018. Printed in USA.

ISBN 978-1-7753259-3-2

(electronic version)

CONTENTS

	Introduction	1
1	Chapter 1 Things to consider once you get a ticket	5
2	Chapter 2 Types of offences: strict, absolute and mens rea	14
3	Chapter 3 Offences Ontario Canada example of how this applies: speeding, stop sign, improper left hand turn, seatbelt, careless driving, drive under suspension, drive no insurance, drive no insurance slip, fail to sign in ink, drive hand held device (cell phone), no ownership, parking tickets bylaw,	25
4	Chapter 4 Summary apply it to your own State, country.	58

Introduction:

So, you are concerned about a ticket that you or someone else has received. You might be preparing a certain case for an appeal because of some error in law that you believe had taken place at your trial. If you have questions about anything concerning your decisions about what to do or how to go about dealing with your ticket or trial then this is the right book for you. The website feasteasylaw.com is also available to you as a compliment to this book.

The first thing you must do is think about whether you FEEL as if you are deserving of the ticket or in other words whether you should have gotten your ticket or not. Once you have made up your mind then you can begin to look hard into this book along with the website fasteasylaw.com and see what your options are. The idea behind fighting your ticket in court is to determine whether you or not you will be found guilty of the charge or not. So, the idea of how you feel about whether you deserve the ticket or not is something entirely different. Yes, these are two different things. You can feel as if you are deserving of the ticket or not but it is an entirely different thing as to whether you will be found guilty of the charge or not if you take your matter to trial. Many people are deserving of their tickets yet they often are successful at fighting their tickets.

Whether you choose to fight your ticket or pay it is entirely up to you, and no one else. The issue is that what you require before this decision is made is the right information an that's where this book and website fasteasylaw.com comes into the picture. Research always takes time but this is all be done for you. So, let's get started.

Chapter One:
Traffic tickets the three things to consider:

You have received the ticket or tickets from a police officer or some other government authority and now you have to consider what is happening to you. What you may also have to consider is how those that are insured along with you are going to be affected as well. It is a decision that not many people take consideration of until they have been given the infraction notice such as a speeding ticket. Realistically, not many people are well prepared for the experience even if they have received a ticket in the past and there is no reason why you should blindly trust a representative who you hire to represent you in court. You should know what you are getting into and what the law says before you hire anyone to represent you. This allows you to be informed, ask the correct questions and seek the correct answers. Why trust some who you think is good or says, as I have heard many in the past say that they know people. That to me means that they have just blindly handed over their money. It also means that they are not informed yet if they were they would probable do a better job at representing themselves in court. You must be aware of three things right off the bat, for example if you have received any traffic violation:

1. Insurance premium are going higher
2. The amount of the fine of the ticket or tickets

3. Your demerit points

Depending on the ticket the penalties may be severe such as driving privileges being suspended.

Most important consideration: Think about it for a minute; there is obviously always an actual cost for going to court; such as your time or the time you might spend on a representative. As we can see from above, there is also a cost for not having a trial- you have to pay for the ticket (if you don't then your driver's license is suspended and you will have a harder time getting around day-to-day). It's going to cost you either way a certain amount of money. Do you think your own time and stress is not worth anything? Get control of the situation right away, as you have done by purchasing this book and reviewing fasteasylaw.com, because it is your problem and you are facing it right now. Ok, enough with the pep talk, let's get down to business but all of this had to be said to get you into the right state of mind. The problem is that many people are so uniformed about their situation it is regrettable when they have so much information that is available to them yet until now, people involved in the business have made it so difficult for people to come to an understanding with their own situation and I blame court staff, lawyers and paralegals. It is similar to when you have gotten your first job and the one training you makes the job out to be so difficult yet after a while you realize how easy it really is and do you know why? It is only because those on the job need to look good themselves and make the boss feel as if they are the only one's who are good enough to do the job and not you. Same situation when it comes to fighting your ticket, those in places of authority have to made to look important so that they can continue. This does not mean that there are not good lawyers out here, but this does not mean that you are incapable of grasping the concepts yourself. Traffic court or these lower courts are actually designed to be accessible, which means they are suppose to be able to be managed by people like yourself, alone and without representation.

Go to fasteasylaw.com and each of these three categories are listed on the bottom part of the home page for you to review-diligently updated.

Insurance premiums

How many tickets that you have on your record for the last three years. This is the primary concern for insurance companies and you can check this by obtaining a driver abstract from the ministry of transportation for approximately 12 dollars. Another primary concern, is whether you have an accident that was your fault, then the problems become worse. Note: There are some insurance companies that offer forgiveness for the first of your accidents (check with your insurance broker). Finally, some insurance companies take into consideration on how many times you or anyone under your policy has taken out a claim such as a broken windshield in assessing the cost of your insurance premiums (again check with your broker as to whether this may be a mitigating factor). From the point of view of insurance companies, they want your money but don't want to have to pay out, so the best rates are going to those who never claim and never have traffic infractions. This is quite a low percentage of the people who are insured as you can imagine. And, one last point to remember is that new the driver the more expensive the insurance premium, so, a brand-new driver who within the first three years of receiving their drivers license is susceptible to higher insurance premiums and the threat of obtaining a traffic ticket that will raise their premiums even higher.

The fine

Each type of offence carries with it a fine and is noted on most tickets. For more serious offences the fine is not noted but a automatic summons to court is recorded on offence notice that you receive which generally carry higher amounts of fines. Fines themselves are subject to the courts discretion, which means a justice or judge can substantially lower or raise a fine to a maximum amount if they feel that it is required. Finally, there are options available to the defendant that allow the to ask for time to pay the fine. They can ask for 6 months or more and then re-apply to the court for more time if they have tried to make payments (generally- something must be paid) in order to ask for more time to pay. This will allow the defendant to keep their licenses from going under suspension for nonpayment of the amount of the fine of the moving violation.

Demerit points:

A specific number of demerit points is allotted to particular drivers. This all depends on your location so check with your city, state or province. Again, you can attend the DMV, MTO or ministry of transportation and obtain a driver abstract to see how many you have. This number will decrease depending on how many tickets that you receive that carry demerit point reductions with them. For example, speeding 20 KM over the posted speed limit carries a 3-point reduction to your driver's license. For example in Canada this means that you will lose three demerit points for 2 years from the date that you either pay the fine, if you choose not to go to trial or are convicted a trial for the offence. Check ministry website for your specific city, state or province. In Canada, after two years then these points automatically return.

NOTE: As in Canada these demerit points automatically return and in some locations in the USA you can attend specific classes to reduce demerit point loss, but not in Canada. The offence itself In Canada, will only automatically come off your abstract after three years. From the day you pay or get convicted of your offence is when 3 years begins before the come off your driving record.

Let's review:

Price of your **insurance** that you must pay for a certain time (in Canada its at least the next three years at least, accidents that were your fault stay for 6 yrs) involves:

> After any two tickets on your driving record

> Another factor depends on how many accidents or claims that are your fault which you have

> In either of these cases the insurance company has the right under law to drop you from their insurance. Bang, you're on facility. This means a very high premium. Your premium can be affected by others insured in your household as well under your policy

You should always call various insurance companies or brokers at random to see for yourself. Here are degrees of severity to consider when dealing with insurance companies. One ticket will take you to higher premiums one most insurance companies but any two and over will definitely cause higher premiums. Any accident at your fault will also increase your chances of a higher premium.

Price of fine: this will affect your pocket book and failure to pay some fines could get your driver's license suspended and if you get caught driving under suspension then you open yourself to the possibility that you could go to jail if you are caught driving while suspended. Collection agencies are separate entities and it is recommended to always pay your fine at court house to get a receipt of payment (very good idea).

> This is a court house issue. The fine must be dealt with at the court house.

> The fine does not affect your credit rating. If a collection agency gets involved, if you do not pay the fine with them - deal with the fine at the court house, you can ask for extensions of time to pay your fine there if need be.

> There are some traffic violations that will not suspend your driver's license if not paid.

Ministry of transportation (Ontario but also applies to all provinces in Canada) demerit point system

Points: these affect your ability to drive if you accumulate to many point reductions then you can lose your ability to drive (if you receive too many reductions in points). From the time you receive the ticket from the officer is when for example in Canada the 2 years start for the demerit points return back to you. Similarly in all common law jurisdictions.

> Police pulled you over and gave you a ticket. Whether you go to court or not, the ministry calculates 2 years from this day that the officer gave you the ticket.

> If you win in court the demerit points don't get taken away. If you lose then the ministry goes back to the day you received the ticket in all common law jurisdictions.

> The demerit point system is a ministry of transportation thing not a court house thing to consider (this only changes if you plea to a different charge with prosecutor at the court house to a different charge). If the prosecutor at the court house wants to change a charge to a charge that has no points; this is done before trial. The justice of the peace or magistrate cannot change this.

Court house fine must be paid and should be paid at any court house in the province where you obtained the infraction (ticket or violation).

Chapter 2:

Types of offences all common law jurisdiction including U.S.A, Canada, Britain, Japan etc. (France is civil but a similar understanding applies)

Understanding this chapter will show you what you can argue or say to the court to fight your ticket

You must locate the type of offence that you have to see what types of defence's or excuses are allowed at trial. In other words, this means there are specific things that you can say to the judge, magistrate (justice of the peace) at court during your trial. Some things will be allowed at the trial part and the other will be able to be said at the sentencing if you are found guilty. Link up the infraction that you have with what type of offence it is either absolute strict or means rea. Then under the type of offence your charge is you can only use certain defenses to the charge and there is no other way to proceed. You have to work within these guidelines.

Strict liability offenses:

Must prove beyond a reasonable doubt that the defendant committed the illegal act.

The prosecution must prove or establish this first. See, [crowns case for proving it was you either on fateasylaw.com and under summary in this book](). To prove that it was you there must be a witness such as the police officer or another independent (or other person) witness and they must testify that it was you.

Once this is proven then negligence is presumed meaning that the court looks at you as guilty and it is on you to prove now (when its tie for you to present evidence) that you are innocent. So, you are assumed to be guilty unlike when you first walked into the court room you were presumed innocent. Do, you see how things just changed under strict liability offences.

You have the burden of now proving to the court that you are innocent by rebutting the prosecutor's evidence- proving that it is unlikely what the prosecutor is saying by putting the evidence on (the prosecution puts their evidence on first) is true.

Alternatively, if you give an excuse: If when you put on your evidence and you use an excuse then the court asks itself what a normal person would do give similar circumstances. If a normal person (reasonable person) would have done the same thing; being confused or getting the wrong information at no fault to yourself, then the court will find you not guilty. So, let's say that you paid your insurance up to date and received no notice that you were canceled. The court may find you innocent of the charge of driving with no insurance if the insurance company canceled your insurance without your knowledge.

By giving an excuse you are now establishing to the court that on a balance of probabilities that you were not negligent: You took all reasonable care to avoid the act. And, court will base their ruling on whether the court feels that you are honest or not. The defense of due diligence. You have the burden of doing so, and the court asks itself what a normal person would do give similar circumstances.

Subjective fault meaning whether you knew or not that what you did was wrong or the factors that led to the offence were wrong. But, given some circumstances if these were true then it would have made what you did right.

You base this on a defense of what is called due diligence or reasonable mistake of fact.

The defendant must prove on a balance of probabilities (that means given all of the things that took place) that you took reasonable care not to commit the illegal act.

That they made a reasonable mistake of fact if true would have rendered the acts lawful.

Due diligence:

There will be specific actions that you did which make the case for due diligence. Some form of Reasonable foreseeability will be expected. Reasonable in this case means hindsight. So, if you are asking the court to believe your story then the court will consider whether a normally reasonable person in society would have done the same as yourself in the situation that you were in and determine if you should have seen that you were going to have this problem. In other words, whether you should have seen that this may have happened. Not 100 percent but some high degree that you should have seen what was going to happen as a result of your actions.

Mistakes of fact:

Mistake of fact must be reasonable. Usually, the defendant must prove that they took all reasonable steps and made all reasonable inquires to determine the correct information. In other words, I did it, I was aware of the risk but I took due care. Morally innocent. The defendant must have made a mistake of fact honestly and that there was a good reason for it-reasonable grounds for the mistake. Mistake of fact:

Note: Referring to sec 80 of the POA- see fasteasylaw.com links under provincial offences act Ontario under common law defence's. This section states that judge made law referring to absolute, strict and means rea defence's apply in provincial court and section 81POA points out that ignorance of the law is not an excuse.

If the defendant honestly believed in certain facts if true would have rendered his or her actions legal then the defendant did not intend to commit the offense-rebutting the presumption of intending the natural consequences of their actions. By rebuttal, what is meant is that if the crown prosecutor puts on a case showing that it was you who committed the act then in strict liability cases you may counter the crowns case by using the defense of mistake of fact.

If the defendant honestly believed in certain mistaken facts but not that they shut their mind to the truth or were 'willfully blind' to the truth then this may be enough to successfully defend your case.

Examples of some common strict liability offences under HTA: or see fasteasylaw.com

Strict liability infractions or these types of offences violate the presumption of innocence. So, once the prosecutor or crown identifies that it was you who committed the act then it is up to the accused or you who must prove that they were not negligent in allowing a harmful or dangerous act to occur. Normally, strict liability offences are created when public safety is a concern and not just a way from the government to impose a fine. You will often hear a judge or magistrate talk about the dangers associated with these offences.

Absolute liability offenses

The prosecution must prove beyond a reasonable doubt that the defendant committed the offense or act(s).

No proof is required of any additional fault element- guilty knowledge or negligence. A due diligence defense is unacceptable here and it is enough that you were identified as the one who committed the offence. An absolute liability offense can punish those who did not intend to commit the act and those who take all precautions reasonable not to commit the act (punishing the morally innocent.)

How to tell if it is an absolute liability offence: Absolute liability is determined if, the provincial offense clearly excludes the defense of reasonable care and clarity indicates that the guilt requires only proof of the illegal act. See fasteasylaw.com under links in Ontario for Speeding under HTA sec 128.

Defenses to absolute liability are: involuntariness, causation and necessity

How the court examines legislation to determine the type of offence it is:

The court will determine the intent of legislation taking into consideration the regulatory pattern adopted by legislation or the purpose of the statute, legislative history, relationship to other provincial laws. The will often look at the importance of the penalty- its harshness, difficulty with complying with legislation. The precision of language used and if it specifically seems to reject of reasonable care defense in its wording. The court will (or should) examine the effect on the defendant's charter of rights. If the infraction is one of absolute liability and the legislation states that there is a possibility of prison to the charge then the defendant may consider challenging the law as unconstitutional (simply because absolute liability charges should not have imprisonment attached to them). Be prepared for the crown to try and reinterpret the offense as strict liability so that it remains constitutional.

In other words, As in Canada the legal reference is that if an absolute liability offense breaches sec 7 of the Charter and if the court finds that it is not a reasonable limit under sec 1 of the charter, then by sec 52(1), the offense is unconstitutional and of no force and effect. See fasteasylaw.com for sec 52 (1) of the Constitutional act 1982 under links. In other common law jurisdictions different sections apply stating a similar feature.

Examples of Absolute liability offences: See fasteasylaw.com for complete list.

Speeding

Fail to stop for red light

Stop sign

Defence's under absolute liability:

Causation defense:

This means that if the crowns case cannot attach the physical action by you to the act then they have not shown cause

And you tell the judge before you give your side of the story that you would like this case dismissed at this point because the crown has failed to show cause. Or attach you to the offence.

The crown must fail to prove this if you use this defense:

The crown must prove beyond a reasonable doubt that the defendant caused the illegal act. There must be proof of actus reus or physical action element to the offense. Causation is the relationship between the defendant and the illegal act or acts which resulted. Not necessary to prove that the defendant was the sole cause of the illegal act or acts. It is enough that they contributed to the illegal act or acts and that their contribution was outside the de minimus range.

Involuntariness defense

To an extent the illegal act or acts must be voluntary and within the control of the defendant.
-If someone drugged you

-If someone took over control where you could do nothing about it
Necessity defense:

You must have these elements

1. Must be an imminent risk that the defendant must avoid an imminent peril
2. Must be no other reasonable legal alternative to the course of action taken by the defendant
3. The harm that was caused by the defendant must be less than the harm avoided
4. The emergency may not reasonably be foreseeable

Onus is on the defense (or you) to prove an emergency existed and then it becomes the crown who must prove that the necessity excuse does not apply in your case. Imminent peril and no reasonable alternative are evaluated on modified by an objective standard, considering the characteristic and situation of the defendant in light of what a reasonable person in society would do. So, the court will look at your situation and see whether it was proportional of what a reasonable person would have done in your shoes.

Mens rea offences:

This is what is often known as the courts consideration of a guilty mind. Here the prosecution must prove beyond a reasonable doubt that the defendant did commit the offense or act. (Prove that it was them). And that the defendant had a particular state of mind. The court can determine the state of mind by examining the defendant's intent, knowledge or recklessness. These things can be determined if the defendant may make an admission as to their state of mind. So, if you say that at the time this is what you were thinking then the court will often accept this unless you are unbelievable or if other evidence is put forward that counters what you are saying. What the court does is utilize what is often called the common-sense principal which states that people normally intend the natural consequences of their actions. Intension means that the defendant intended to bring about certain results or that they intended to commit the act

What knowledge the defendant had may be considered in fairly limited circumstances by the court to determine how your actions were affected by what you knew. For example, in a criminal case where the defendant is accused of aiding in a murder it will be a question for the court to determine if the person knew that the person murdered was going to be murdered.

Recklessness means that there was a risk of certain behavior then acting on it was unacceptable disregard to that risk. If you were reckless in your actions then the court will tend to lean that you intended the act to happen.

While there may be few types of Highway traffic offences that involve means rea these are most notably:

-Failing to stop for police

-Avoiding police while being pursued

Quick summary for all three types of offences:

Mens rea offences in which the Crown must prove the actus reus as well as
some positive state of mind such as intent, knowledge or recklessness;

Strict Liability offences in which the doing of the prohibited act, prima facie,
imports the offence, leaving it up to the accused to avoid liability by establishing
that he took all reasonable care; and

Absolute Liability offences where it is not open to the accused to exculpate
himself by showing that he was free of fault.

Canadian caselaw reference for what constitutes certain types of offences or how the court interprets legislation. Similarly as it is in all common law jurisdictions it is the common law or case law that dictates the type of offence. In France and civil jurisdictions see both statue and case law.

Case: Mr. Justice Dickson found that public welfare offences would, *prima facie*, be classified as strict liability offences. The Crown is required to prove the *actus reus* of each offence beyond a reasonable doubt. If the Crown is able to do so, then in accordance with the direction of the Supreme Court of Canada in Sault Ste. Marie (*supra*), in order to escape conviction, the onus devolves upon the defendant to satisfy the court, on a balance of probabilities, either that he had an honest but mistaken belief in facts which, if true, would render the acts innocent, or that he exercised all reasonable care so as to avoid committing the offences.

Canadian example

In Levis (City) v. Tetreault, [2006] S.C.J. No. 12, the Supreme Court of Canada
explained the Sault Ste. Marie decision with respect to the application of due diligence
in the following words:
"Under the approach adopted by the Court, the accused in fact has both the
opportunity to prove due diligence and the burden of doing so. An objective standard
is applied under which the conduct of the accused is assessed against that of a
reasonable person in similar circumstances. Alternatively, in order to avoid being convicted, the defendant must satisfy his burden, on a balance of probabilities, that an authorization, exception, exemption or qualification prescribed by law operates in his favour. In this regard, section 47(3) of the P.O.A., provides as follows: The burden of proving that an authorization, exception, exemption or *qualification prescribed by law operates in favour of the defendant is on the defendant, and the prosecutor is not required, except by way of rebuttal, to prove that the authorization, exception, exemption or qualification does not operate in favour of the defendant, whether or not it is set out in the information."*

Chapter 3:

For example how this works: Offences
Ontario Canada: See how this works.

Apply chapters 1 and 2 to your own jurisdictions in the way it is applied for Canada. These are general offences that will similarly fit in your area. For Canadians, Americans and internationals whom have received tickets driving in Ontario this applies exactly.

Speeding ticket:

General description:

Absolute liability. You were charge with going over the posted rate of speed. In other words, you were going too fast and the police officer caught you. There are then two key points 1. The police officer registered some way that you were going at a certain speed and 2. The posted speed was so much. Now, since you were given the ticket or summons to court this is the evidence against you. People rarely break it down in these simple terms. They know that this is what had happened but in breaking it down in this way it makes it clear. Yes, you can say that you knew that you were speeding but now you want to know how to beat the charge. Well then you must understand that this is the evidence against you.

If you want to fight the ticket then everyone wants to know how to I beat the police officers evidence.

The answer is that you do not. The evidence before the court if you take the matter to trial is substantial. Meaning, you have to understand that the courts and the police hear these charges almost every day and hear all of the excuses. So, what you have to do is not come up with an excuse but a legitimate defense.

This type of offence is called and absolute liability offence unless; you were charges with speeding under stunt driving. So, no excuse will get you off the ticket no matter what you have hear through other people, you cannot say to the court I was speeding but…

Ontario Canada: Description of speeding under stunt driving:

If you were going over 50 km of the posted speed then you were charged with something called stunt driving. If it involves speeding and stunt driving has many categories for it, speeding is just one of the reasons why you can be charged with stunt driving. See stunt driving for further details

The types of speeding tickets:

If you received a ticket and it is speeding under the community safety zone then the fine rises and demerit point reduction is same.

Legislation (The Law)

See under H.T.A. section 128 absolute liability. If stunt driving then H.T.A. Sec 171 strict liability.

Penalties or fines

The fines very here and you should refer to the speeding chart. As for stunt driving the penalties can be fines upwards of 10,000 Canadian dollars, driving license suspension of minimum to year and jail time. Refer for fines to the H.T.A. sec 171. All of these will show up on your abstract. The demerit points you should also refer to the chart for speeding depending on how fast you were going.

What to do or options

Generally, the crown prosecutor will normally drop the rate of speed to a lower amount depending on the rate of speed. For a full description of this you must enter our pay part. Normally the courts will reduce the speed to a lower amount and this reduces the fine and the demerit points involved.

Stunt driving (speeding):

For stunt driving if the court lowers the speed under 50 then it becomes a simple speeding ticket and stunt driving no longer will show up on your drivers abstract. A 7-day suspension of you driving privileges applies immediately once you are charged. To get that off if you were found not guilty of stunt driving you must see our pay part. Towing and impounding of the vehicle for 7 days is applied to you immediately as well. Further your license privileges are suspended for 7 days and this suspension shows up on the abstract as soon as you get charged. To get this off if you are found not guilty.

Crown or prosecutor must prove only that you were speeding: That you were speeding and that it was you.

This is done by the cop giving evidence that a. he pulled you over got your license or knew that it was you somehow and identifies you in court. Then b. the evidence is based on the radar gun or a pace by the police vehicle. The majorities of the new police cruisers are equipped with measuring devices on the front and back of the cars now that can measure your speed. They must state the place and a rough time that it happened and the posted speed limit where they clocked you. Then the case is proven and it is for the defendant to prove otherwise.

So, you can argue against those two things to break the crowns case. Not impossible but note that the crown succeeds 99 percent of the time-don't believe otherwise.

WARNING: If you are told by a friend that they have this person who gets them off speeding tickets all of the time it is a strong possibility that this is a scam. The courts are not in any sort of financial difficulty and if you think for a second that there are people out there higher than our court system; think again. Only if the police officer does not show up or the disclosure is not ready or if there is a defect on the ticket do people get other people off speeding charges relatively easy- basic technical issues.

Some possible excuses (and excuses don't work for absolute liability speeding offences under sec 128 HTA) that people may relate to:

-I was speeding but I have a good reason for it

-I was overtaking a vehicle by passing so I had to increase my speed

-I though the speed limit was higher I did not see sign.

-My speedometer was reading a speed that the officer was claim was higher

-I know I wasn't speeding just because I know what a certain speed feels like

-Other cars were going faster than me

-I know that the cop clocked another car in front of me and not me

And none of these work with absolute liability charges, but you may ask yourself if the police officer lost sight of you and if so then the crown may have a hard time proving it was you, even if the officer lost sight of you for a brief moment. You can argue that they did lose sight of you and this brings in doubt that it was you who committed the offence.

If the radar gun was working (officer did the checks as specified by radar gun manual), if the cop paced you with their car and the last time the police car was serviced was not to long ago, if there are no major mistakes on the ticket itself such as wrong date, if you have ordered disclosure and have received it, then it will be very difficult to beat a speeding ticket unless you can bring evidence that contradicts what the police officer is saying (see the officers notes). If the police officer begins to have independent recollection or in other words begins to remember things about that day that are not on their notes and you can directly contradict them then this brings doubt. But, because the police officer has so much experience with writing tickets it may prove too difficult for you to have a trial and in this case, you may find that it's in your interest to make a deal to a lesser charge.

Note: If the police officer brought down the rate of speed that you were traveling and you have a trial then the crown can re charge you under the original higher rate of speed.

Deal on speeding tickets:

Can only deal before the judge hands down there ruling normally can only make a deal before you actually have your trial. Before trial on the day of your trial you can still deal.

1-15 over is demerit no point reduction

No deal

16-30 over is 3 demerit points

Deal to lesser charge no points

31-49 over is 4 point demerit

Deal to 3 or no points

Stunt driving is 50 and over

Here 4 points by lowering the speed is the proper deal

These are all based on the co-operation with the crown. This system differs from country, province and state. For example check DMV or ministry in your jurisdiction for demerit point reduction.

Disobey Stop sign:

Description

Absolute liability. This means that the police officer saw that you did not come to a complete stop at a stop sign. If this involves an accident then someone who may not be the police officer had to have seen that you entered the intersection without stopping (independent witness).

Legislation (The Law)

See H.T.A. sec 136(1)(a) fasteasylaw.com under links for HTA Ontario (or HTA for the province that issued the ticket)

Penalties and fines

The general fine is approximately $110.00 including victim fine surcharge and the demerit point loss are 3. See fasteasylaw.com for HTA legislation and then ministry of transportation all under links for demerit point. There is a victim sur charge attached to the fine (this is attached to all fines which is generally a small amount that is added to the original fine)

What to do

You can generally walk in to the crowns office by having a resolution meeting and see if the crown will offer you a charge that is anything less than the

3 demerit points that you are already facing. Generally speaking the crowns office will not normally reduce the ticket to a charge that carries no demerit points on this offence without a really good defense. But the crown may offer you 2 demerit points and a fine. If you choose to take the deal then they can deal with the whole process that day. If you like at this time you can refuse the deal and still have a trial date.

Trial:

Generally, order disclosure, and go over the officer's notes. If you did come to a full stop and not a rolling stop, just take the stand, making sure that you are truthful and believable and state to the court that you did come to a full stop. It becomes the officer's word against yours and you will be surprised that often the judge or magistrate will believe you allowing you to escape conviction.

Improper left hand turn or turns not in safety

Brief description of the offence and reference to the appropriate legislation.

- Strict liability offence, see sec 142(1) and 144(8) HTA see fasteasylaw.com links HTA

The majority of these offences involve a collision. The main theme for this is discussing the charge itself, while the relevant case law involves collisions at trial independent witnesses must be called by the prosecution. If the witnesses fail to attend trial then the prosecution may more than likely fail in proving its case. It may be the case that one or more witnesses do not show up and in this case the prosecutor must decide whether they have enough to proceed or not. This is relevant because the police officer, nine times out of ten was not a witness to the collision. It may be the case where the police office just happened to be there but not in the majority of the cases and they can only attest to what they did and what witnesses may have said.

Ministry of transportation demerit points

- 2 demerit points Ontario
- Confirm with appropriate ministry of transport in province by finding it on webpage under favorite links
- Courts do not concern themselves with demerit points and cannot give the defendant

the opportunity to pay the fine or a higher fine if convicted of the offence

See location for link to MTO on website fasteasylaw.com, once you have located the link you may search for the corresponding demerit point loss for the offence. In Ontario the **demerit point loss is 2**. The ministry of transportation only deals with licensing and they are the ones who determine the demerit point loss not the court house. The court house is only concern is the offence and penalty in the form of a fine.

Seatbelt

Description:

This offence is an Absolute liability offence. This means that the officer charged because A. you were not wearing your seatbelt all together, B. you were not wearing it properly, which could mean a lot of different things or C. you were not wearing the seatbelt fully only part of the seat belt. This refers to those seatbelts normally that come in two parts like the seatbelts in the driver side of the car.

Legislation (The Law)

See H.T.A section 106 under fasteasylaw.com use links to find H.T.A. (search for other provinces is available here)

Penalty and fine

The total demerit points taken off you driver's abstract are 2. The fine is just over $100.00 Canadian dollars.

What to do or options

Exemptions Medical:

If you have a doctor's note that exempts you from wearing a seat belt this must show that on the date in question; means the day you were pulled over, the doctor gave you a letter that says that you were unable to wear a seatbelt for reasons of a medical nature. To note this letter must be in car or if you are exempt but generally the prosecutor will throw it out if you present it to them.

This can be done by way of a resolution meeting. See resolution meeting with prosecutor.

Exemption as a type of driver:

As a driver for some type of work that you do – see H.T.A. as long as you were wearing it in the prescribe place and time you should not have gotten the ticket. See H.T.A. to see if you are exempt. For any of these reasons they should dismiss the charge. These methods are easily dealt with by way of a resolution meeting. If the prosecutor at that time does not want to throw out the charge then you will have to have a trial. If the prosecutor at the time of the resolution meeting offers you a deal to the lesser charge and you fall into one of these exemption categories then you must review our pay part of this website.

Inoperable or your seatbelt wasn't working at the time:

If your seatbelt was not working seeking a deal is recommended because it is you as the driver who is at all times responsible for the workings of your vehicle. You should view our pay part for details on this. But the prosecutor has the option during the resolution meeting or the trial to offer you the deal of inoperable seatbelt. This is just s fine and it does not show up on your drivers abstract.

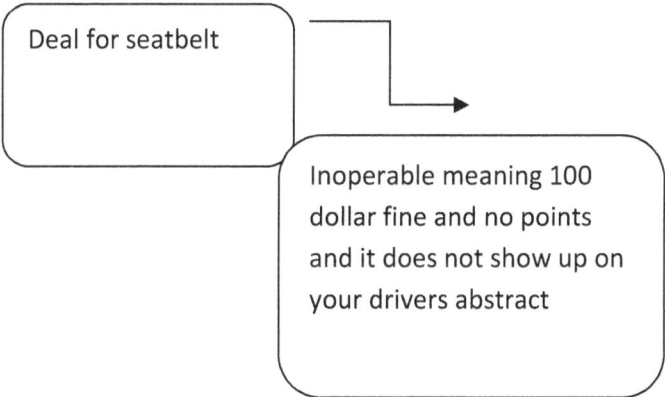

What the prosecutor has to prove:

The police officer has to attend and give evidence a. that it was you he identified normally this is done by you giving him your license and then b. then he must say that it was you who was not wearing the seatbelt.

Careless driving

Description of charge:

This type of charge is called **a quasi-criminal charge and here the courts are generally looking for recklessness in your actions to determine the fault element**. This charge means that you were driving in some careless manner and your intention or state of mind is in question here. Normally it involves an accident. If you were you involved in an accident, this means that the crown must subpoena the people that were involved in an accident with you. If you were not involved in an accident then the police officer was a witness to your actions or some witness who was there. The key to these charges is that someone witness you do something that was improper.

Legislation (The Law)

Ontario- See The H.T.A. and section 130. Fasteasylaw.com under links for legislation in your province. Careless driving reference is posted on home page at bottom right.

Penalties and fine:

This will show up on your abstract if you are convicted of it and it carries 6 demerit points against your driver's license. See the legislation above for the penalties involved. As for the amount it carries a fine upwards of $400.00 Canadian dollars. What is possible as a penalty under this act is a fine up to $1000 and a jail term of no more than two years in severe cases. See legislation above for further details.

Options what to do

The majority of this charge depends on the circumstances involved such as:

> The result:
>
> What happened?
>
> Did you have a duty of care?

> Actions you caused.
>
> And what you did.
>
> Did this constitute negligence?

Any deal that the crown prosecutor would offer depends on the circumstances normally these are left for those who were involved in an accident. Not anyone tells you the circumstances that constituted this charge are unique to every individual. If you rear ended a vehicle, if you hit something and there was no other vehicle involved, if you caused an accident and were making a left turn.

Trial

Important is that the witnesses attend. If there are no witnesses or there are witnesses that the crown is dependent upon for there case then the case will be dismissed if the witness or witnesses don't show up. Yes, the police officer has to show up as well. The crown can ask for an adjournment to another date and you can object. If an adjournment is granted then have the justice of the peace make it preemptory on the crown. This means that the crown witnesses have to show up the next time or another adjournment will not be granted for them. Object if the crown asks for it to be preemptory on you saying that they have no reason to have this granted because you were here ready to go. You see you go up to the prosecutor and see if the witnesses are there before the trial begins and they have to tell you before you make any deals.

What you have to prove:

Is that you were not reckless or due care in what you did. For example. were you careful in your actions as not to cause and accident? You may have made a mistake but you were not necessarily reckless in so far that you could have foreseen what had happened. The court must consider certain things and one of the is what a reasonable person would have done in your situation. If you can show that your actions were reasonable, for example such as you took all reasonable care when you made a lane change or you took all reasonable care as you passed a car on the road, then the court may not find that you are guilty of careless driving. Much of the trial is based on what the witnesses say and what you say. Very rarely do the police reconstruct the sense of the accident and give a detailed report. If this happens, you must rebut what the police are saying which is normally done by hiring your own independent authorities that can challenge the reconstruction of the accident as the police officers are portraying. How do you know if this type of evidence is being offered? By ordering disclosure and if its not there then they wont be offering it as evidence. In the disclosure you will be able to see the witness statements and this will help you enabling you to see what the witnesses are claiming against you. Normally, the witnesses have to state evidence that clearly shows that they saw what they saw. So they cannot be standing behind a tree and expect the court to believe that hey saw what they say they saw. Finally, if it involves and accident then the person or persons who were involved in the accident must be present. The crown can often proceed with their case if one of the persons involved in the accident shows up. The oldest trick in the book is that defendants keep asking for adjournments so that the witnesses don't show up. Yes, this can happen but be careful don't upset the court by making unsupported requests for adjournments.

Drive Under suspension

Description

Strict liability. This means is that you were charged with driving while you're driving privileges were suspended. This can happen from either a court order that prevented you from driving or by not paying your fines.

Legislation (The Law)
See H.T.A. sec (53); see fasteasylaw.com under links for legislation and penalties in the province that you received the offence.

Penalties and fines

If it was your first time then you will have a minimum fine set by the court and your driving privileges will be suspended for an additional 6 months. You do not loose demerit points here.

What to do

The question is basically that do you have a defense for this charge. It normally is the case that people forget to pay their fines then have their driver's license suspended unknowingly. Here you can attend court and show that you paid the fine arguing that you had no idea that you were suspended and this likely will case the charge to be dropped. But, if it was because of a court order that stopped you from driving it is quite another thing. These charges normally boil down to the answer to the question did you know that your license was suspended?

The suggestion is that if you have a reasonable excuse for this charge then you can explain it to the crown prosecutor on the day set on the summons that your received and it may be possible for the crown prosecutor to offer you a lesser charge of drive with no license.

Drive with No Insurance

Description
This is called a **strict liability offence**. This charge is clear the owner of the car must maintain proper insurance on the car. There may be various reasons why you should not be charged for this offence but the reason why you were charged is that the police officer felt that you had not insurance on the car.

Legislation:
Ontario- See C.A.I.A. sec 2: fasteasylaw.com links

Penalties and fines
Ontario- This offence if convicted does show up on your drivers abstract. The penalties vary for people who were charged from the first time to many other times. For this information specifically check the legislation. The minimum and maximum fines can begin at $5,000.00 Canadian dollars, but normally with the proper circumstance the court will take a lower fine into consideration maybe$ 1,000 or$ 2,000 Canadian dollars for a first offence. If you wish to plead guilty to this charge see the pay part and review sentencing.

What to do

There are no deals to change the charge to something else that is not as severe as this charge. The only thing that you can do is talk to the crown prosecutor about the fine; if they will agree to an acceptable amount. You must consider a trial and fight the charge in order to win by providing one of the defenses under strict liability. If you find that you have no defense to the charge you can try to reduce the penalty by stating to the court your financial situation and circumstances as to why you felt that you needed to drive. Often enough people use the excuse that they needed to go to work but this is not a factor that the court will consider in reducing your fine. You need to show financial hardship. It all depends on the justice of the peace of judge and how they see fit to set a fine and how long you have to pay.

No Insurance slip

Description
Absolute liability. Basically, you were not able to present the officer with a copy of your insurance slip that means that you may have had an outdated slip with you as well. Your insurance slip should reflect the date that the police officer had pulled you over. Either the slip or proof of insurance was not in the car or you couldn't find it in time to show it to the police officer. You have insurance this is not a charge where the cop is accusing you of not having insurance.

Legislation:
See the C.A.I.A for the exact legislation. Sec 3(1). Fasteasylw.com under links for legislation and fine.

The penalties
This carries no points but does show up on your drivers abstract (will affect your insurance). It carries a small fine of under $70.00 Canadian dollars.

See exact pricing under legislation under links as fasteasylaw.com under compulsory automobile insurance act or CAIA.

What to do: Deal normally automatic
If this was your only charge then ask the court to set a resolution meeting or to set a meeting with the prosecutor instead of a trial date. Once you set this meeting bring the copy of the insurance slip with you and show it to the crown prosecutor. This is

where they should dismiss the charge. If you have more than one ticket then your opinions would then be to deal with them all here. If you are fighting it you must go to the pay part, at trial.

- See getting more than one ticket.
- See resolution meetings.

Drive Hand Held Communication Device

Description

Absolute liability. This is a charged normally reserved for those people who drive while talking on a cellular phone. The police officer observed that you were operating the phone in one hand while you were driving. This is not a charge that involves those people who have a hands-free device.

Legislation (The Law)
See H.T.A. sec 78 (1)

Penalties and fines
The fine is generally $155.00 including the surcharge. And carries no demerit points and does show up on your drivers abstract.

What to do
The courts have been quite clear that they will not reduce the charge to another charge that carries another name. generally, the courts will only let an individual talk about the fine that they are going to receive. You must consider fighting this charge at trial if you want to have the charge dismissed.

Improper left turn

Description

This is a charge that involves you making a left hand turn when you should not have. This charge also can involve an accident. In which case it would involve witnesses to the fact that you made the improper left-hand turn

Legislation

See H.T.A sec

fine and penalty

The penalty for this $100.00 Canadian dollar and carries a demerit point loss of 2 points.

What to do

You can generally talk to the crown prosecutor and see if they will change the charge in making a deal for some other charge that carries no demerit points.

No Ownership

Description

The reason why you received this ticket was that you did not show the officer the ownership of the vehicle. This is the general reason; that this is what the police officer asks when a person gets pulled over and this documentation was not shown to the police officer.

Legislation (The Law)

- See Highway Traffic Act or H.T.A... See Sec 7 (1) (a) of the H.T.A.

Penalties

This carries a fine and no demerit points. It does not show up on your drivers abstract. It is a fine of approximately $100.00 Canadian dollars.
- See drivers abstract for description of what this is and how to use it.
- See exact pricing of fine.

What to do (your options)

Generally, if you attend the court house and show the prosecutor the copy original of the ownership they will dismiss the charge. If you have more than one charge, see more than one charge. You can attend the court house and ask for a resolution meeting. Generally the prosecutor will want all of the charges dealt with on that day so do not assume that if you have more than one ticket that the prosecutor will drop the one charge of no ownership and then you can go to trial on the other one or other tickets that you received that day.

- Resolution meeting
- More than one ticket received
- See trial in the pay part for this ticket if going to court to fight it.

Deal automatic

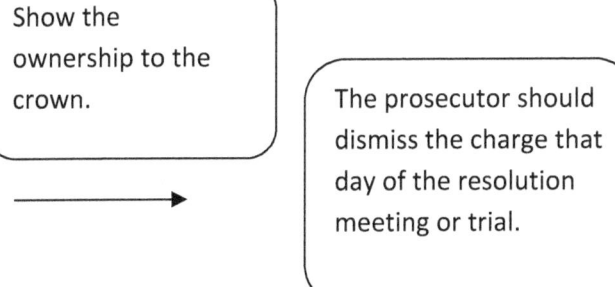

Fail to sign permit in ink

Description
This means that you do not have a signed ownership. You as owner must have been charged with this charge. Being charged and not being the owner see our pay par to fight the charge. The ownership must be signed by the owner in ink not pencil.

Legislation (The Law)
See H.T.A. sec 628(8)(1)

Penalties and fines
The fine imposed is just over $100.00 Canadian dollars

What to do
Normally, the matter can be resolved by making a resolution meeting with the crown prosecutor and showing them the ownership is now signed in ink. This is such a frivolous ticket that the crown may just withdrawal the charge (no conviction and no fine) once you have shown them that it is signed.

Parking tickets and Bylaw infractions:

If there is any mistake on the face of the ticket and that can amount to a name being improperly spelt or an incorrect address then these types of tickets are dismissed. Unlike, traffic violations both Bylaw and parking tickets must show all of the correct information on its face or in other words they must have all of the correct information printed on the ticket itself.

These are all absolute liability offences and as such must show by a witness that the infraction was committed by you. In the case of some bylaw infractions that involve property, then the property owner may be held responsible for an infraction. As such it is on the property owner to deal with the ticket or face a fine. Similarly, the owner of a vehicle is responsible for a parking violation and it does not matter who was driving the car or in care of the vehicle.

Chapter 4:
Summarize

Let's Summarize thus far for all traffic tickets:

We have an idea that the police officer has given you the ticket for the offence of drive without wearing proper seatbelt assembly. It is a strict liability offence and you have a demerit point loss along with a fine. Some people make the mistake and think that because demerit point loss is a bad thing that it is something that the court has control of. The court does not set them so if you are convicted of the offence the points go along with it as does the fine. The fine is also set but given certain circumstances of monetary impairment that you may have the court will consider reducing the fine. The court can also give more time to pay the fine. In some cases the court can give a defendant up to 90 days to pay the fine.

Paying the fine:

- Pay fine at any court house that deals with traffic tickets and keep the receipt for your records
- Pay online refer to where on webpage fasteasylaw.com

This can be done at any court house that deals with traffic tickets. You should also keep the receipt for your records. Often, they may be a mistake and a fine can come back to haunt you although you have paid the fine. A collection agency may call and you will have to provide them with proof or they will not stop harassing you. The court house is run by human beings remember and sometimes they make mistakes. The volumes of tickets that the court office administrators handle can be quite high so do always keep your receipts.

Information on the ticket:

The ticket itself has a bunch of information on it. See fasteasylaw.com for ticket info and what it means

What you must consider in choosing your options:

- Choose to either pay fine, resolution meeting with crown or trial
- Factors are insurance premiums, fine and sentence, demerit point loss and the time and effort that you will have to put into dealing with offence

Definitely consider the truth of whether you think that you are guilty of the offence or not and then consider the issue of whether you can be found guilty or not in court. These may be two different things

You may be concerned solely with winning the ticket at all costs but we first must be realistic. There is no sense walking into a situation that you will lose no matter what gimmicks people throw at you. So the first thing you must ask your self are you guilty of the offence or not. Once you have admitted to yourself which category you fall into from the two. Then you can begin to make an informed decision.

Referring to the webpage you can HERE put the part of the website. You must consider the options that are available to you and paying the ticket may be the easiest thing for you to do. The ministry of transportation holds the information on your record for 3 years from the day you are convicted of the offence. By paying the ticket and not making a trial date or resolution meeting the day you pay is the day that becomes your conviction date. If you fail to pay the fine and take any action by making a trial date or a resolution meeting with the prosecutor, then the court will convict you on their own. Whichever option you choose it should be made within 15 days of receiving the ticket.

The insurance companies determine whether or not to raise your rates, depends on how many offences are on your record. You can obtain a copy of your driving record or drivers abstract from the ministry of transportation near you for a moderate fee. This is advised. The norm is that you do not want 2 tickets on your record or else you run the risk of higher rates. Other determining factors are how many accidents you may have that are your fault. Insurance companies normally keep these on a central database for all other insurance companies to see for 6 years.

Always good to check drivers abstract:

1. Check how many tickets are registered against your record for the last 3 years by going to the ministry of transportation and obtaining a copy of you drivers abstract.
2. Consider how many accidents that you may have against you that are your fault

Some people do not consider that they may get another ticket in the near future and that if they drag out the process by taking it to court it can only hurt them. They may get another ticket and go to trial and get convicted. Then they have another ticket take that to trial and get convicted within a year's difference. Then they have 2 convictions on their abstract for the next 3 years. In other words, it is always advisable to consider and way out what will happen in the future. It may have been an option that they make a resolution meeting with the prosecutor as soon as possible to see if they may get away with having the court agree to a lesser charge that is not as damaging and severe. For example, a person may receive a ticket of 30 over the posted rate of speed. The resolution meeting may be set and the prosecutor, hopefully in a good mood that day reduces your ticket to 15 over the rate of speed. The points are removed and the fine is greatly reduced. The insurance company will now only see a small traffic ticket and not a high one such as 30 over.

The insurance companies are funny beasts. They are a corporation and are concerned with making money. They set policies in place and do determine that bigger tickets turn into bigger money. Often it is the case that if a person has two tickets on their record for 30 over the rate of speed the insurance company has cause to raise their rates considerably. If that same insurance company sees that there are two 15 over tickets on the persons abstract they will not raise that person's rates as high. Unfortunately, only the insurance companies can answer that question of which is better or the same. Demerit points do not always mean more money for your insurance company but it is often the case that nobody knows until it is too late the answer to this question. It is always advisable to seek the best resolution possible for the outcome of your court case. If you know you chances are slim then take the deal and get it over with.

Deals or resolution meeting with the prosecutor before a trial date:

- Example: Do you have a doctor's note or are you exempt from wearing seatbelt?
- Inoperable seat belt is a lesser charge with no demerit points that a prosecutor may consider
- In Ontario only for now you may have a valid or reasonable excuse although there is no hard-case law at moment to refer to for

what is a valid or reasonable excuse for not wearing your seatbelt?

These deals are often struck at trial but they can be done easily by setting a meeting first before setting a trial date. You have the option here to discuss with the prosecutor what option they may offer you instead of going to trial. The courts are encouraged to do this. It saves time and money for the court and its shows that you want to deal with the matter right away not wasting the courts time by having a trial and the justice of the peace may be more lenient with you and consider lowering the fine considerably.
Unfortunately, it may not be the case where the prosecutor offers you any respectable deal. For this charge of seatbelt, an excellent deal would be to give you what is called inoperable seatbelt.
If you have a doctor's note or are exempt from driving with a seat belt this is a good opportunity to either show the prosecutor that you have a doctor's note and for some reason did not provide it to the police officer or tell the prosecutor that you are exempt by law from wearing a seat belt. HERE show where on act you are exempt. The prosecutor once they are made aware of this may drop the charge then and there.

Review one more time:
1. A good deal is inoperable seat belt that carries no demerit points and does not

appear on your drivers abstract. So insurance does not see it.
2. If you have a doctor's note and show it to the crown they should drop the charge. That doctor's note must stipulate that you are unable to wear the seat belt for some medical reason. That dates of the letter must correspond to the dates that you got the ticket.
3. You should way your options to see if you want to make a deal and resolve your issue sooner than going to trial.
4. You can always go to trial if this deal does not suit you.

What the crown or State must prove:

The prosecutor must prove that beyond a reasonable doubt that you did what the offence or ticket says. You can think of it as pointing the finger at you. This is done by bringing the officer to court to testify that they say that they saw you not wearing your seatbelt. The way that they attach you to the offence is simple that the police officer saw you. The police officer will have to take the stand and stipulate that that is what they saw. This is why if the officer doesn't show up the case may be dismissed if the prosecutor doesn't ask for an adjournment. (See Here adjournment requests) You may as the defendant order disclosure, to see how the officers note are written. Why this is important is that if there was a tree in the way or some obstruction and if this is not written in there notes then you can bring it up and argue that they police officer could not see you. Pictures will only strengthen your case.

If the ticket was issued in Ontario according to recent case law this is a strict liability offence and you can give the court good reason why you were not wearing your seatbelt. If the ticket was in another province other than Quebec then because the case law is relatively new; you should consider the offence as an absolute liability charge and you cannot give a reasonable excuse to the charge.

What the defendant must prove

We must examine this offence in 2 ways. The defense can make an argument if they are outside of Ontario that the court should follow the recent case law in Ontario where the higher court has ruled that it is a strict liability defense. (HERE put motions on how to do this). If the defendant is in Ontario then this foundation has already been done and you can now give a defense of due diligence
If a court outside of Ontario does not follow the trend of the Ontario courts then we are dealing with the category of absolute liability. The courts here will not accept an excuse to the charge. The defendant cannot say I was not wearing my seat belt but…As soon as the defendant says that they were not wearing the seatbelt, the case is over.

First as a strict liability offence:
What were the circumstances? In the more recent case R v Wilson 2013 ONCJ, the defendant was explaining to the court that he had stopped at a stop sign and took his seatbelt off to pick something up. At this time, it seems that the police officer observed the defendant and the defendant was not wearing his seatbelt. The reason why you were not wearing your seatbelt is unique to yourself. Someone or something could have caused your seatbelt to have come undone. This is something that is out of your control. A third category is that the seatbelt was not working properly. If you can prove that the seatbelt broke during driving and there was nothing you could do about it then you have another reasonable excuse.
The most effective reason is the reason that is the truth. It is a proven fact the more a defendant tries to lie on the stand, the worse the outcome at trial is.

Three basic categories:

1. You have just taken your seatbelt off for one moment. It was safe to do so and you felt that it was necessary to do so. The issue you must think of is was it really safe and was it really necessary to do so? These questions are easily answered by you.
2. Someone maybe a friend in the back seat of your car had somehow removed your seatbelt
3. The last one would be that for some reason the seatbelt failed to work while you were

driving. Notice that it is not that the seatbelt was not working and you still chose to drive the car. This would imply that you knowingly knew that the seatbelt was not working yet still drove despite this issue.
- The first category is where you feel that your reasoning was sound why you took your seatbelt off for a moment.
- The second is where you had no control over not wearing your seatbelt
- The third is where the seatbelt stopped working properly.

As an absolute liability offence:

The defendant cannot say that they were not wearing the seatbelt without losing the battle unless you fall into the defense of necessity.
A second defense for this offence may be a causation defense where the crown fails to prove their case by being unable to prove that through proper identification that it was you who committed the offence. This will depend on the officer's testimony which is generally summarized in their notes which they may refer when they provide their testimony in chief on the stand as the prosecutor or crown asks them questions (and may use them when you ask them questions).

Crown must prove that the officer or witness saw you in the act of breaking the law.

In Conclusion:
So, if you have read all of the above information you now have knowledge and are able to make an informed decision regarding:

1. The legislation and demerit points
2. The category that your offence falls into
3. From this we know that your defense has to fall into a category and you can give a reason for what happened
4. From all of this you can figure out if you want to go to court and have a trial or not
5. You now make a rational decision is it better to pay the fine or try to deal
6. You can always SET A TRIAL DATE AND TRY A DEAL THERE IF YOU CHANGE YOUR MIND.
7. Order the disclosure – officers notes-see Fasteasylaw.com.

Next step:

If you have opted for trial and you are not represented by a lawyer then the court will be or is supposed to be more lenient on you because of it. In other words, the justice of the peace does not expect you to have the same knowledge as an average lawyer so they will allow you more grace when you are trying to make your case. But, the amount of curtesy or leniency varies between courts.

Canada only but see if your constitutional rights were violated in any state in America this applies or in European union see ECHR: In Canada if there are no 'fatal errors and a in Canada a Charter argument or challenge does not apply to your specific case (such as if there was a great enough delay to your trial, you may argue that your Charter rights were violated under section 11(b)) then you must rely on one of the defence's available to you given your offence or take a plea deal or be found guilty. The 11(b) argument is available on our website fasteasylaw.com and all you have to do is answer certain questions and the computer program fills in and prepares the paper work for you. All you have to do is print it off and submit it to the court to initiate your Charter challenge that it took to long to go to court. This service is available for any charge throughout Canada. So, you can use the 11 (b) argument here for anything including criminal charges.

Trial:

Remember you must figure out what the prosecutor has to prove:

The police officer has to attend and give evidence a. that it was you he identified normally this is done by you giving him your license and then b. then he must say that it was you who was not wearing the seatbelt. What the crown case is going to consist of is that the officer after stating that they saw you and noticed that you were not wearing your seatbelt. After the officer identifies you then it is case over. The defense cannot come up with an excuse to the charge. The crown will ask you on the stand a direct question-were you wearing the seat belt or not? Once you answer that you were not wearing the seatbelt the case is over in the crowns eyes. The defense must now avail itself of a defense that fits in the scope of absolute liability. Or the defense must avail them of what might exempt them of the charge under legislation such as having a doctor's permission in the form of a note. Or that the seatbelt did not work and the question now becomes up to the crown to show that the police officer checked that it did not work. This needs to be developed.

What are you circumstances?
You were not wearing it at the time
You had just taken it off to do something
You were only going from one place close from where you were
It seatbelt doesn't work.

Will give appropriate answers to all of these circumstances.
Sentencing see sentencing general.

What we need is the caselaw and then the case law discussed here. It is what they are arguing if they are going to make a detail case then so be it. We can make this very involved in arguing what the police officer has in their notes.

www.ingramcontent.com/pod-product-compliance
Lightning Source LLC
Chambersburg PA
CBHW031126160426
43192CB00008B/1130